INTRO:

He can barely walk.

He can barely talk.

He runs a country.

Joseph Robinette Biden Jr. was born on November 20, 1942, in Scranton, Pennsylvania, to Joseph Biden Sr. and Catherine Eugenia Finnegan. He grew up in Scranton and later moved to Delaware with his family when he was 10 years old. Biden graduated from the University of Delaware with a double major in history and political science and later earned his law degree from Syracuse University.

Biden's political career began when he was elected to the New Castle County Council in 1970. In 1972, at the age of 29, he became one of the youngest people ever elected to the United States Senate. However, tragedy struck shortly after his election when his wife, Neilia, and their daughter, Naomi, were killed in a car accident. His sons, Beau and Hunter, were seriously injured but survived. Despite this personal loss, Biden decided to serve in the Senate, commuting daily from Delaware to Washington, D.C., to be with his sons.

During his time in the Senate, Biden focused on issues such as criminal justice, foreign relations, and combating violence against women. He chaired the Senate Judiciary Committee and the Senate Foreign Relations Committee, playing a key role in shaping U.S. policy on crime, immigration, and international affairs.

In 2008, Biden was chosen by then-Senator Barack Obama as his running mate in the presidential election. The Obama-Biden ticket won the election, and Biden served as Vice President of the United States from 2009 to 2017. During his tenure as vice president, Biden played a significant role in shaping the administration's domestic and foreign policies, including the passage of the Affordable Care Act and the implementation of the economic stimulus package in response to the Great Recession.

In 2020, Biden ran for president for the third time, securing the Democratic nomination. He campaigned on a platform of unity, empathy, and restoring the soul of the nation. In the general election, Biden defeated incumbent President Donald Trump and became the 46th President of the United States. He was inaugurated on January 20, 2021, at the age of 78, making him the oldest person ever to assume the presidency. Throughout his career, Biden has been known for his bipartisan approach to politics, his commitment to public service, and his dedication to his family.

"Don't underestimate Joe's ability to f–k things up," as President Obama said during Biden's campaign for the 2020 Presidency versus Trump.

Our country is in a downward spiral, and in this book, you will see why. The individual running our beloved United States of America is barely capable of taking a shit and wiping his own ass. Excuse the vulgar language right there; I'm only talking the way our President Biden does when he gets angry, and well, I'm angry.

With the double standards in politics, Republican Presidents don't get the same leeway Democratic Presidents and Democratic nominees for Presidents get. Take into consideration the 2016 Democratic nominee for President, Hillary Clinton. She got a "get out of jail free card" for mishandling classified information/files and lying about the usage of those files on a private computer server located inside of her private residence (a clear violation of Federal law).

People grow old and start to lose their true self. We have seen this play out in public in the last five years.

For example, actor Bruce Willis produced and starred in movies while affected by a cognitive disease, Aphasia.

After his removal from the spotlight and the bad press received by those around him for the downward spiral of his creative works, the truth was finally revealed.

For years, his family, associates, and business partners shielded the outside world from knowing, yet pushing his products and advertisements. Now that it's not a secret anymore, you have friends, actors he worked with, and producers who all claim that they saw the signs of his cognitive decline.

Once President Biden leaves office, a tell-all will be released detailing his diseased brain, the memory loss from the diseased brain, and how the White House, the United States Government, and his friends and families played into the act, keeping it a secret. President Biden has an onset of a cognitive disorder or disease. I am not a doctor, but common sense prevails in this argument.

The facts presented in his book all point to a cognitive decline that can't be overlooked anymore.
Signs of cognitive decline:

1. Problems recognizing friends and family members
difficulty with language and problems with reading,writing, or

working with numbers

2. Difficulty organizing thoughts and thinking logically
inability to learn new tasks or to cope with new or unexpected situations.

3. Inappropriate outbursts of anger
perceptual-motor problems, such as getting out of a chair or tripping and falling randomly.

By the end of this book, you'll be flabbergasted at the masses that prop up President Biden as a coherent person. When President Biden makes a public mistake, the crowd either laughs or claps; they will change the topic completely and move on. The enablers are like a sitcom audience: zombies, motionless in thought.

Look at how they enable the President, for they are responsible for treason, manipulation, and the downfall of the United States.

Democratic Sen. Chris Coons of Delaware, a co-chair of President Joe Biden's reelection campaign:

"As you well know, small gaffes are a part of what all of us in public life do," Coons said in an interview with ABC News.

Several voters interviewed by CBS News said Biden's mistakes make him more relatable.

"So what? I do , too," said Will Cokley, a general manager and South Carolina native living in Charlotte who came to see Biden in Rock Hill. "He's human. It makes him real, not scripted."

"There are more important things to worry about than Biden's gaffes" - Johnathan Capehart

Source: Washington Post

Does the United States population care if President Joe Biden is mentally unfit to do his job? During a 2021 update on the President's health, CNN published a report that showed the President didn't complete a cognitive abilities exam.

During an interview with CNN's Anderson Cooper on Anderson Cooper 360, Gupta was asked if President Biden had taken any type test for mental capabilities.

"It doesn't seem like it," Gupta replied. "I read pretty carefully through the doctor's report and they mention neurological exam, but that was more in terms of testing motor strength and sensation and things like that."

"As far as we know, for President Biden, we didn't see any kind of test like that performed," Gupta added.

They stand with President Biden. They endorse him. They adore him. They enable him.

PHYSICIAN TO THE PRESIDENT
THE WHITE HOUSE

28 February 2024

MEMORANDUM FOR: KARINE JEAN-PIERRE
                         ASSISTANT TO THE PRESIDENT AND
                         WHITE HOUSE PRESS SECRETARY

FROM: KEVIN C. O'CONNOR, D.O., FAAFP
                         PHYSICIAN TO THE PRESIDENT

SUBJECT: President Biden's current health summary

As requested by the patient, the following is a summary of the current health status of President Joseph R. Biden. The President feels well and this year's physical identified no new concerns. He continues to be fit for duty and fully executes all of his responsibilities without any exemptions or accommodations.

As in previous years, I have conducted a comprehensive review of President Biden's medical history and performed a detailed physical examination. This physical has again included specialty consultation with several of our Presidential Specialty Consultants from the Walter Reed National Military Medical Center. These specialties have included Optometry, Dentistry, Orthopedics (Foot and Ankle), Orthopedics (Spine), Physical Therapy, Neurology, Sleep Medicine, Cardiology, Radiology and Dermatology. Each of these specialists have independently reviewed the chart, examined the President, and concur with my findings and recommendations. I have also solicited feedback from my respected colleagues – the other physicians in the White House Medical Unit, who see the patient every day. Each of these doctors has reviewed my report for accuracy. My conclusions have been further informed through discussions with several of my fellow professors from the George Washington University School of Medicine and Health Sciences.

This document updates my last statement, from 16 February 2023. Today's memorandum speaks to the President's current health and fitness and addresses any interval change.

Summary

This patient's current medical considerations are detailed as above, and remain stable and well-controlled. They include obstructive sleep apnea, a-fib with normal ventricular response, hyperlipidemia, gastroesophageal reflux, seasonal allergies, spinal arthritis and sensory peripheral neuropathy of the feet. For these, he takes three common prescription medications and three common over-the-counter medications.

President Biden is a healthy, active, robust 81-year-old male, who remains fit to successfully execute the duties of the Presidency, to include those as Chief Executive, Head of State and Commander in Chief.

Respectfully submitted,

Kevin C. O'Connor, D.O., FAAFP
Physician to the President
The White House
Associate Professor, The George Washington University School of Medicine & Health Sciences

(President Biden can't remember anything anymore, not even the names of those who stand beside him).

CHAPTER 1: A HISTORY OF GAFFES

President Biden's memory has been fading for a while. The last fifteen years have showcased a cognitive decline that mimics the onset of Alzheimer's disease or a similar disease.

Stage 1: Before Symptoms Appear

Just like with many diseases, changes in the brain that are related to Alzheimer's begin before symptoms are noticeable.

"This time period — often called 'pre-clinical Alzheimer's disease' — likely begins 10 or 15 years before people have symptoms," says Dr. Wolk.

Source: Pennmedicine.org

BEFORE PRESIDENCY:

I have arranged articles and headlines during President Biden's tenure as Senator and Vice President. These include a history of "off-the-wall" comments and memory lapses that will give you a better understanding of his current cognitive state.

Senator Biden comments on Senator Obama.

In 2007, Biden called Barack Obama the first "mainstream African-American who is articulate, bright, clean, and nice-looking guy," adding, "I mean, that's a storybook, man."

Senator Biden tells a paraplegic to stand.

During a 2008 campaign rally in Missouri, Biden asked the audience to applaud State Senator Chuck Graham.

Vice President Biden: "Stand up, Chuck, let 'em see you."

Graham, a paraplegic following a car accident, is confined to a wheelchair.

Source: News Week

Vice President Biden mourns death of someone who's alive.

March 23, 2010:

"It's not even surprising anymore when the Vice President says something impolitic, is it? A week ago, during a White House St. Patrick's Day celebration, he briefly mourned the death of the Irish Prime Minister's mother, even though she was very much alive."

Source: TIME

Vice President Biden tells a false story.

Presidential hopeful Joe Biden is on the defensive after reportedly mistelling a story on the campaign trail about a heroic Navy captain. Biden has been telling some version of the story for years.

"This guy climbed down a ravine, carried this guy up on his back under fire," the former vice president said during a campaign stop in New Hampshire last week.

"The general wanted me to pin the Silver Star on him. I got up there, and this is the God's truth, my word as a Biden. He stood at attention. I went to pin it on him. He said, 'Sir, I don't want the damn thing. Do not pin it on me, sir. Please, sir, do not do that. He died! He died!'"

But according to the Washington Post, who spoke to more than a dozen military and campaign sources, "Biden got the time period, the location, the heroic act, the type of medal, the military branch and the rank of the recipient, as well as his own role in the ceremony" wrong.

Source: Washington Post

Vice President Biden makes off-hand comments about race.

The Vice President shrugs off his tendency to shoot from the hip. In May, he said, "No one has ever doubted I mean what I say. The problem is I sometimes say all that I mean."

Tuesday marked the third time since the spring that Biden has made comments that needed to be cleaned up.
In August, Republicans and some Democrats were outraged when Biden made this reference to an audience of African-Americans:

"He's going to once again let the big banks once again write the rules. Unchain Wall Street. They're going to put you all back in chains."

Vice President Biden can't remember that Margaret Thatcher is dead.

In 2019, for the second time, President Biden corrected himself when he referred to Margaret Thatcher, who died multiple years ago and was the last prime minister 30+ years ago. President Biden was actually referring to Theresa May.

Source: Axios

Vice President Biden goes off with his remarks and makes no sense.

In March 2020, Vice President Biden talked about COVID and stated this:

Vice President Biden: "We cannot let this, we've never allowed any crisis from the Civil War straight through to the pandemic of '17, all the way around, '16, we have never, never let our democracy take second fiddle, way they, we can both have a democracy and ... correct the public health."

Vice President Biden says you're not black if you vote for Donald Trump.

In 2020, Charlamagne told Biden that he should come to the studio in New York City for another interview, telling the former vice president that "we've got more questions."

Vice President Biden: "You've got more questions? Well, I tell you what, if you have a problem figuring out whether you're for me or Trump, then you ain't black."

<u>Vice President Biden makes a verbal mistake or is telling the truth?</u>

In October 2020, Vice President gave a speech and said this:

Vice President Biden: "We have put together, I think, the most extensive and inclusive voter fraud organization in the history of American politics."

CHAPTER 2: THE MEMORY FADES

Once the memory fades, the person fades, their legacy fades, and they are seen as a fragment of their former selves. Their agendas of the past and their hope for the future die when they die.

I've assembled news articles and have watched hundreds of videos to showcase President Biden's fading memory during his Presidency. Below are news articles, observations from videos (written in script format), and journalistic sources that confirm that President Biden is a false vessel, corrupted by those around him, with no thought process.

President Biden gives a speech and talks about how he makes mistakes often while he gives his speeches.

President Biden: "Once every once in a while - I make a mistake not like once in a while, speech, but anyway years ago when I started talking for this job I said please take your seats and there weren't any seats; everyone was standing, there were no chairs."

President Biden mixes up his birthday age.

In an interaction with reporters after undergoing his first routine physical in office, the oldest president in American history said that he is going to celebrate his '58th' birthday while it was his '79th' on November 20 in, 2021.

President Biden mixed up the dates on where he was on September 11, 2001.

Biden took flack from Americans who lost loved ones in the September 11, 2001, terrorist attacks by observing the 22nd anniversary in Alaska instead of at one of the tragic sites.

That would have been bad enough, but the president made it worse by falsely saying he'd been to Ground Zero on 9/12.

President Biden: "Ground Zero in New York — I remember standing there the next day and looking at the building. And I felt like I was looking through the gates of hell," Biden told US troops in Anchorage.

However, Biden's own memoir placed him in Washington, DC the day after 2,977 people were murdered by 19 Al Qaeda terrorists.

The White House, not for the first time, stepped in to do clean-up, claiming Biden was actually referencing a visit he made with a delegation of senators nine days after the attacks.

Source: New York Post

In a speech, Joe Biden has one single word to define America.

President Biden: "America is a nation that can be defined in a single word, (slurring) asufutimaehaehfutbw"

15

President Biden makes a mistake by referring to Vice President Kamala Harris as something different than her title.

President Biden: "There's been a little change in arrangement of who is on the stage because of the first lady's husband contracting COVID. But look at this room and what you see -- (Biden recognizes he made a gaffe).

(Gestering toward crowd).

President Biden: That's right. She's fine. It's me who's not together. Secondly, The First Gentleman. How about that?"

President Biden refers to Vice President Harris as President Harris at a speech.

President Biden: "President Harris is here to make sure we do things the right way."

President Biden again refers to Vice President Harris as President.

President Biden while delivering a speech at South Carolina State University during its 2021 Fall commencement ceremony called Vice President Kamala Harris, President.

Biden refers to US Vice President Kamala Harris as "President Harris."

President Biden: "All kidding aside, of course, President Harris, who's a proud Howard alumn, might have something to say about Delaware State."

Source: Wionews.com

President Biden shakes the hand of... nobody.

President Biden: "God bless you all."

(Biden finishes his speech and walks to the right of the podium. He reaches out for a handshake, but no one is there. He stands for five seconds and then makes his way to the back of the stage.)

President Biden gives a speech and goes off sentence when he can't finish it.

President Biden: "Best way to get something done, if it holds near and dear for you, if you'd like to be able to... anyway."

President Biden reads a teleprompter while giving a speech and reads the ending of the script.

President Biden: "Because of the actions we've taken, things have begun to change, end of quote."

President Biden gives a speech and refers to former President Trump as Congressman Trump.

(Referring to jobs)

President Biden: "Instead of cutting them, like Congressman Trump and Bogart want to do."

President Biden talks about the women on his staff but isn't

clear on what he means.

President Biden: "More than half the women in my cabinet, more than half, more than half the people in my cabinet, more than half the women on my, uh, administration are women."

President Biden gives a speech and brings up the number of hours and times and isn't clear on what he's referring to as he looks confused.

President Biden: "Sixty-eight times, sixty-eight hours, sixty times, more than sixty-eight hours."

President Biden almost introduces himself in his speech.

(Biden walks up to the podium to introduce himself but then notices he doesn't need to, and there's Someone there to introduce him as President Biden at the "Bidenomics" speech.)

President Biden: "Good afternoon, folks; I'm not introducing myself; Mark is."

President Biden mixes up words at the end of a speech and makes a sentence out of a fragment.

President Biden: "Thank you all, God bless you all, let's go..."

(Pauses).

President Biden: Let's go late, lick, the world; let's get it done."

(Smiles).

President Biden says, "Happy Thanksgiving at a Christmas event decorated with a significant background for Christmas.

President Biden: "Happy Thanksgiving, see ya'll."

(Notices the decorations around him).

President Biden: "Oops."
(Looking at microphone).

President Biden: "Who am I giving this to?"

President Biden, in Bidenomics speech, gives a confusing explanation of how the middle class was built.

President Biden: "The middle class was built by the middle class. And the unions built the middle class."

President Biden gives a speech at APEC: CEO SUMMIT 2023.

(Squinting eyes to read teleprompter)

President Biden: "Leading executives, leading tech, companies, like (inaudible and looking confused), and I'm going to mispronounce; I'm not even going to try."

President Biden forgets Declaration of Independence Quote:

During a speech in March 2021, President Biden stumbled over a portion of the Declaration of Independence, saying:

President Biden: "We hold these truths to be self-evident, that all men and women are created equal, endowed by their Creator, you know, the thing."

While he quickly corrected himself, the moment garnered attention and criticism.

President Biden can't recall the name of his Secretary of Defense.

March 8, 2021:

President Biden: "And I want to thank the sec — the, the, ah former general -"

(Biden confused while Vice President Harris rolls her eyes).

President Biden: "I keep calling him general, but my, my — the guy who runs that outfit over there."

President Biden, at a "200 million COVID shots given event speech," gets his words mixed up.

April 21, 2021:

Pressident Biden: "The receptiveness, the saloon, the salon, maybe going to the salon. I don't know."

President Biden goes off track while introducing his guests at a speech.

May 28, 2021:

Presidential Remarks at Joint Base Langley-Eustis Military Base:

President Biden: "I'm especially honored to share the stage with Britney and Jordan and Nathan and Margaret Catherine. I love those barrettes you have. I tell you what. Look at her. She looks like she's 19-years-old. Sitting here like a little lady in a race car. Britney, you're doing triple duty."

Source: C-SPAN

President Biden went through a major memory lapse during a virtual online meeting High Holy Days meeting with Jewish Rabbis.

September 2, 2021:

Biden stated he visited the Pittsburgh congregation where, in 2018, 11 people were slain in the nation's worst anti-Semitic hate crime.

President Biden: "I remember spending time at the, you know, going to the, you know, the Tree of Life synagogue, speaking with them."

The next day, the White House had to admit that Biden made the story up.

Biden struggled with his memory throughout the virtual meeting with the rabbis. "My mind is going blank now," he said as he fought to recall details of his daughter Ashley's 2012 wedding.

Source: New York Post

President Biden can't recall the Australian Prime Minister's name.

September 15, 2021:

President Biden: "I want to thank... uh..."

(Pauses for two seconds).

President Biden: "That fella down under."

(Pauses for one second).

President Biden: "Thank you very much, pal."

(Looking confused).

President Biden: "Thank you, Mr. Prime Minister."

President Biden mixes up the years.

January 4, 2022:

Pressident Biden gave a speech about the availability of COVID shots.

President Biden: "There's a lot of reason to be hopeful in 2020, but for God's sake, please take advantage of what is available."

President Biden mixes up Ukraine and Iran.

March 2, 2022:

During the State of the Union President Biden tried to give credit to Ukraine during his first State of the Union speech, but accidentally praised Iran instead.

President Biden: "Putin may circle Kyiv with tanks," the president declared, less than a week after Russia launched its invasion. "But he will never gain the hearts and souls of the Iranian people."

Vice President Kamala Harris, seated behind Biden on the dais of the House Chamber in the US Capitol, appeared to grit her teeth and whisper "Ukrainian" President Bidencontinued.

President Biden misstates words during a speech on green energy

March 31, 2022:

President Biden: "If your home is powered by safer, cheaper, cleaner electricity, like solar or heat pumps, you can save about $500 a month on average," Biden said as he touted Democrats' green energy proposals.
Hours later, the White House quietly corrected the official transcript of the president's remarks, crossing out the word "month" and inserting the word "year" in its place.

Source: New York Post

President Biden tries to sound like a badass targeting Russia but fails to pronounce his words correctly.

April 28, 2022:

President Biden: "I'm also sending to Congress a comprehensive package of — that will enhance our underlying effort to accommodate the Russian oligarchs and make sure we take their — take their, their ill-begotten gains. Ha, we're going to 'accommodate' them." (Laughing at his own slip up).

President Biden: "We're going to seize their yachts, their luxury homes, and other ill-begotten gains of Putin's kleptocrac- — yeah … (Looks confused and for his handlers) Kleptocracy and klep- — the guys who are the kleptocracies."

Source: New York Post

President Biden forgets he's President.

May 2, 2022:

President Biden introduced himself to the crowd at a White House gathering to mark the end of Ramadan.

President Biden: "There have not been many of the senators from Delaware. It's a small state."

President Biden makes a random comment about the Queen of England at the Safer Communities Summit.

July 5, 2022:

(Ending the speech)

President Biden: "God save the queen, man."

(He then points in the direction he thinks he needs to walk toward. Someone offscreen gestures to him that he's correct on the exit).

President Biden gives a speech at a holocaust remembrance and mixes up words.

July 13, 2022:

President Biden: "Keep alive the truth and honor of the holocaust, part of the holo, holocaust. Honor those we lost."

President Biden forgot his friend had died two months earlier and searched for her.

September 28, 2022:

One of Biden's most atrocious verbal misfires in his long career of gaffes came when he sought out Indiana Rep. Jackie Walorski at a White House conference — eight weeks after her high-profile death.

President Biden: "Representative Jackie — are you here? Where's Jackie? I think she was going to be here."

Biden had released a lengthy statement mourning Walorski when she died in a horrific car crash.

His obvious mental fog sparked a reporter revolt at that day's press briefing, as press secretary Karine Jean-Pierre insisted her boss simply had the late congresswoman "top of mind" — but never explained why he thought she was still alive.

"Bless his heart for trying," Walorski's brother Keith Walorski told The Post. "He's forgetful. I don't think anybody would look at the things that he's done and said and say that his mind is as sharp as it used to be."

Source: New York Post

President Biden thinks there are 54 states.

October 28, 2022:

President Biden caused confusion and laughter (they love to laugh when he makes a mistake!) when he said the U.S. had 54 States rather than 50 when speaking about the Affordable Care Act.

President Biden gives a speech regarding Cambodia's Prime Minister and messes up.

November 12, 2022:

President Biden: "Gathered here in Cambodia, I look forward to building, uh, even stronger progress than we already made. And I want to thank the Prime Minister of Col, Colombia's leadership - (notices he made a mistake and starts to move his mouth away from the microphone to address someone offscreen).

President Biden sings happy birthday to MLK III'S wife, Arndrea Waters King and forgets her name.

January 16, 2023:

President Biden: "Happy birthday to you, happy birthday to you, happy birthday dear (mumbles inaudible words), happy birthday to you.

President Biden gives a speech and talked about randomly building a railroad that no one knew about at the League of Conservation Voters gathering.

June 14, 2023:

President Biden: "We have plans to build a railroad from the Pacific all the way across the Indian Ocean."
The real railroad he might have been referring to, according to wral.com:

"The U.S. plans to spend $250 million to support the Lobito Atlantic Railway Corridor, a rail line spanning from the Lobito Port in Angola, which touches the Atlantic Ocean, through Zambia, to the Democratic Republic of the Congo. When we asked the White House about Biden's claim, the press office told us Biden had this railroad project in mind."

President Biden calls Modi the leader of China.

June 27, 2023:

President Biden called Indian Prime Minister Narendra Modi the leader "of a little country that's now the largest in the world, China," before quickly correcting himself: "excuse me . . . India."

Source: New York Post

President Biden mixes up another country into the Russian war with Ukraine.

June 28, 2023:

President Biden was speaking to reporters on the South Lawn of the White House before heading to Chicago when he was asked whether he believed Russian president Vladimir Putin had been weakened by the Wagner Group's mutiny that summer.

He responded by saying that President Putin was "clearly losing the war in Iraq".

Source: Independent.UK

President Biden mixes up who's at war with Russia.

June 28, 2023:

United States President Joe Biden referred to Ukrainian people as Iranians while criticising Russian aggression during his first State of the Union address.

President Biden: "Putin may circle Kyiv with tanks, but he'll never gain the hearts and souls of the Iranian people," Biden said during his address. "He'll never, he'll never extinguish their love of freedom. And he will never, never weaken the resolve of the free world."

Biden walks off interview set before MSNBC host is finished talking.

June 29, 2023:

President Biden rushed off the set of a live television interview on

MSNBC before the show cut to commercial.

The clip of Biden getting up and walking off, shows that his cues and memory are at a loss. His handlers can't control him anymore.

Joe Biden mistakenly states that he has cancer in a speech.

July 20, 2023:

President Biden: "You had to put on your windshield wipers to get, literally, the oil slick off the window. That's why I, and so many damn people I grew up with, have cancer. And why, for the longest time, Delaware had the highest cancer rate in the nation."

The White House issued a statement claiming that President Biden was referring to his history of "Non-Melanoma" skin cancer.

President Biden goes off-cue at a question and answer session at an event in Hanoi, Vietnam, and his aides have to cut it short.

September 10, 2023:

President Biden: "The third world, the uh, excuse me, the third world. The uh, the uh. The southern hemisphere had access to change it, had access to, uh, it wasn't, uh, confrontational at all. (aide cuts him off).

President Biden left Luiz Inácio Lula da Silva visibly agitated after the US president departed a meeting on the sidelines of the United Nations General Assembly without shaking hands goodbye.

September 20, 2023:

That seemingly accidental snub capped off a gaffe-filled appearance in which Biden nearly knocked over a Brazilian flag and was seen fidgeting with his headset device.
"Can you hear me, President Biden? This is a historic moment for Brazil and for the US," asked Lula, the leader of the world's 11th-largest economy, at one point.No answer came as Biden appeared frustrated with his translating device.

"President Biden, can you hear me?"

Biden then nodded along.

Afterwards, Biden shook hands with International Labor Organization Director-General Gilbert Huongbo, who was also onstage, then waved to the crowd and bounced.

Lula was then seen waving an arm in exasperation.

Source: New York Post

President Biden mispronounces the name of a hip-hop legend at an event honoring hip-hop legends.

September 23, 2023:

President Biden: "And two of the great artists of our time represented the groundbreaking legacy of hip-hop in America. LL J Cool J... uhhhhh..."

(looking confused).

President Biden gives a speech in honor of hip-hop artist Queen Latifah and messes up.

September 23, 2023:

President Biden: "With other movies and movies, she earned a Golden Globe and a primetime enemy.

(looking disappointed).

President Biden: "Enemy. That's me."

President Biden gives a speech while confused over the Taylor Swift "Eras" tour going on at the time.

November 20, 2023:

President Biden: "You can say it's even harder than getting a uhh a ticket to the renaissance tour or, or, or -"

(Pauses for two seconds while clinching his teeth and looking off to the left of him).

President Biden: Or Brittany's tour, she's down in; it's kinda warm in Brasil right now."

President Biden gets a "get out of free card" for having a cognitive decline.

Feburary 5, 2024:

WASHINGTON (AP) — A special counsel report released Thursday found evidence that President Joe Biden willfully retained and shared highly classified information when he was a private citizen, including about military and foreign policy in Afghanistan, but concluded that criminal charges were not warranted.

The report from Special Counsel Robert Hur resolves a criminal investigation that had shadowed Biden's presidency for the last year. But its bitingly critical assessment of his handling of sensitive government records and unflattering characterizations of his memory will spark fresh questions about his competency and age that cut at voters' most deep-seated concerns about his candidacy for re-election.

The report described the 81-year-old Democrat's memory as "hazy," "fuzzy," "faulty," "poor" and having "significant limitations." It was noted that Biden could not recall defining milestones in his life, such as when his son Beau died or when he served as vice president.

"My memory is fine," Biden responded Thursday night from the White House, where he grew visibly angry as he denied forgetting when his son died. Beau Biden died of brain cancer in 2015 at the age of 46.

Hur noted that "Mr. Biden's memory was significantly limited" in interviews with the special counsel office as well as with a ghostwriter that Biden worked with.

In his interview with the special counsel's office, Hur writes that Biden twice appeared confused about when his term as vice president ended. The report notes that Biden, who speaks frequently about his son Beau's death, could not remember "even within several years" when he died.

"And his memory appeared hazy when describing the Afghanistan debate that was once so important to him," the report said. "Among other things, he mistakenly said he 'had a real difference' of opinion with General Karl Eikenberry, when, in fact, Eikenberry was an ally whom Mr. Biden cited approvingly in his Thanksgiving memo to President Obama."

Source: Associated Press

██████████████ DRAFT   82

1 [0:44:34.0]

2   MR. HUR: Yes.

3   PRESIDENT BIDEN: And a study where --

4   MR. HUR: Yeah.

5   PRESIDENT BIDEN: -- I would be spending time.

6   MR. HUR: So during this time when you were living

7 at Chain Bridge Road and there were documents relating to

8 the Penn Biden Center, or the Biden Institute, or the Cancer

9 Moonshot, or your book, where did you keep papers that

10 related to those things that you were actively working on?

11   PRESIDENT BIDEN: Well, um... I, I, I, I, I don't

12 know. This is, what, 2017, 2018, that area?

13   MR. HUR: Yes, sir.

14   PRESIDENT BIDEN: Remember, in this timeframe, my

15 son is -- either been deployed or is dying, and, and so it

16 was -- and by the way, there were still a lot of people at

17 the time when I got out of the Senate that were encouraging

18 me to run in this period, except the President. I'm not --

19 and not a mean thing to say. He just thought that she had a

20 better shot of winning the presidency than I did. And so I

21 hadn't, I hadn't, at this point -- even though I'm at Penn,

22 I hadn't walked away from the idea that I may run for office

23 again. But if I ran again, I'd be running for President.

24 And, and so what was happening, though - what month did Beau

25 die? Oh, God, May 30th --

██████████████ **DRAFT** 83

1 [0:46:26.1]

2   MS. COTTON: 2015.

3   UNIDENTIFIED MALE SPEAKER: 2015.

4   PRESIDENT BIDEN: Was it 2015 he had died?

5   UNIDENTIFIED MALE SPEAKER: It was May of 2015.

6   PRESIDENT BIDEN: It was 2015.

7   MR. BAUER: Or I'm not sure the month, sir, but I

8 think that was the year.

9   MR. KRICKBAUM: That's right, Mr. President. It --

10   PRESIDENT BIDEN: And what's happened in the

11 meantime is that as -- and Trump gets elected in November of

12 2017?

13   UNIDENTIFIED MALE SPEAKER: 2016.

14   UNIDENTIFIED MALE SPEAKER: '16.

15   PRESIDENT BIDEN: '16, 2016. All right. So --

16 why do I have 2017 here?

17   MR. SISKEL: That's when you left office, January

18 of 2017.

19   PRESIDENT BIDEN: Yeah, okay. But that's when

20 Trump gets sworn in then, January --

21   MR. SISKEL: Right.

22   MR. BAUER: Right, correct.

23   PRESIDENT BIDEN: Okay, yeah. And in 2017, Beau had

24 passed and -- this is personal -- the genesis of the book and

25 the title *Promise Me, Dad*, was a -- I know you're all --

████████████   DRAFT   84

1   [0:47:55.2]

2   PRESIDENT BIDEN: -- close with your sons and

3   daughters, but Beau was like my right arm and Hunt was my

4   left. These guys were a year and a day apart and they could

5   finish each other's sentences, and Beau -- I used to go home

6   on the train, and in the period that I was still in the

7   Senate -- anyway. (Indiscernible 0:48:27.6). There was

8   pressure -- not pressure. Beau knew how much I adored him,

9   and I know this sounds -- maybe this sounds so -- everybody

10 knew how close we were. There was not anybody in the world

11 who wondered whether or not -- anyway. And so --

12   MR. HUR: Sir, I'm wondering if this is a good

13 time to take a break briefly. Would that be --

14   PRESIDENT BIDEN: No, I -- let me just keep going

15 to get it done. Anyway, here's the deal. Beau -- I used to

16 go home when Beau was at -- from Penn, I used to go home on

17 the train on Fridays and always Jill and I would go -- as

18 the crow flies, Beau and his family lived a mile from where

19 we lived in Delaware. And, and so I'd go home and we'd have

20 dinner together on Friday nights when I'd get home. And my

21 mom, she had died, she had died. Anyway, she had been

22 living with us. And one night, when we were, were having

23 dinner, and Jill came on a different train, she was a little

24 bit later. We had the dinner and Jill said, I'm going to go

25 home and change, which is a mile away, and she left and --

FREE STATE REPORTING, INC.
Court Reporting Transcription
D.C. Area 301-261-1902

████████████████

DOJ-HJC-HUR-0000116

During the interview President Biden couldn't recall any important questions regarding the mishandling of classified documents.

1 [0:31:20.9]

2   PRESIDENT BIDEN: -- "Eyes Only" "Eyes Only."

3 But, it's so easy just to say, anything I write must be

4 "Eyes Only." And 99.9 percent of it has nothing to do with

5 anything I couldn't pick up and read out loud to the public.

6   MR. HUR: Okay.

7   PRESIDENT BIDEN: Am I making any sense to you?

8   MR. HUR: Yes.

9   PRESIDENT BIDEN: Okay.

10   MR. HUR: Understood. So let me circle back now

11 to the questions relating to ███, ███, Michele,

12 ███, those folks who -- maybe I'll describe it as folks

13 who sat at those desks right outside your West Wing office

14 when you were Vice President, that, that group of people.

15   PRESIDENT BIDEN: Okay.

16   MR. HUR: Did you ask those folks who sat at those

17 desks right outside your West Wing office as Vice President,

18 did you ask them to keep -- well -- did you ask them to hang

19 onto classified material that you would like to consult

20 again, and have them maintain it out in their office space?

21   PRESIDENT BIDEN: I don't recall that.

22   MR. HUR: Okay. Do you recall where classified

23 would be kept if you asked your staff to hang onto it?

24   PRESIDENT BIDEN: No.

25   MR. HUR: Okay.

FREE STATE REPORTING, INC.
Court Reporting Transcription
D.C. Area 301-261-1902

1   [0:33:35.9]

2   MR. HUR: -- right now is not about where it was

3   kept, but rather how long --

4   PRESIDENT BIDEN: I have no idea.

5   MR. HUR: -- did your staff know how to hang onto

6   it? Did they have a process where they said, sir, it's been

7   a couple of days, do you still need this?

8   PRESIDENT BIDEN: No. What would happen is,

9   whoever the person who wrote the memo that I want, they

10 would probably come back to say, do you still want to talk

11 about this? That's more likely.

12   MR. HUR: Okay.

13   MR. BAUER: And I just wanted to note, so it's clear

14 on the record, the President just used the word "probably."

15 I mean, in a given day -- I just want to get clear -- he's

16 giving his best recollection of conversations on tons of

17 material that could have come his way, and he would have

18 communicated his preferences and his wishes various -- in

19 various fashion. I just want to make that clear on the record.

20   MR. HUR: Understood. Understood. Okay. So back

21 when the time you were serving as Vice President, sir, did

22 you bring classified material back to the Naval Observatory

23 from the West Wing?

24   PRESIDENT BIDEN: I'm sure I did.

25   MR. HUR: Um-hmm. Can you tell us about what --

███████████ DRAFT 32

```
 1  [0:11:07.5]
 2          MR. KRICKBAUM:  -- arrived.  And in the course of
 3  explaining that memo about Afghanistan, you said to Mark, "I
 4  just found all the classified stuff downstairs."  And so you
 5  can imagine we are curious what you meant when you said, "I
 6  just found all the classified stuff downstairs."
 7          PRESIDENT BIDEN:  I don't remember.  And I'm not
 8  supposed to speculate, right?
 9          MR. BAUER:  Correct.
10          PRESIDENT BIDEN:  So -- okay, well, I don't
11  remember and it may have been -- I just don't remember.
12          MR. KRICKBAUM:  Okay.  Do you remember telling
13  Mark about the handwritten memo that you had written to
14  President Obama?
15          PRESIDENT BIDEN:  I probably did.  I don't
16  remember specifically, but my guess is I may have done that.
17          MR. KRICKBAUM:  Okay.  Do you remember telling him,
18  "I just found all the marked classified stuff downstairs?"
19          PRESIDENT BIDEN:  Marked?
20          MR. KRICKBAUM:  Telling Mark?  Do you remember
21  saying that to him?
22          PRESIDENT BIDEN:  No.
23          MR. KRICKBAUM:  Okay.  Do you remember actually
24  finding any classified stuff downstairs?
25          PRESIDENT BIDEN:  No.  The only thing I can --
```

DRAFT   35

1   [0:40:48.8]

2   PRESIDENT BIDEN: No.

3   MR. HUR: Okay.   One of the things we've learned

4   by speaking to other members of your staff when you were

5   Vice President is that folks in the -- in your national

6   security staff actually kept track of classified binders

7   that had been provided to you, and they tried to track --

8   this one's been returned, but this one has not.   Let's try

9   to find the ones that have not.   Do you recall your staff --

10   PRESIDENT BIDEN: I don't ever recall them telling

11   me they were looking for a binder that I had that they

12   couldn't find.   I don't ever recall that.

13   MR. HUR: Okay.

14   PRESIDENT BIDEN: It could have happened, but I

15   don't recall it.

16   MR. HUR: Okay.   And I just want to make sure that

17   I'm understanding you clearly there.   Do you recall your

18   staff ever coming directly to you and saying, sir, we can't

19   find Binder X, or Binder Y?   Do you know where it is?

20   PRESIDENT BIDEN: I don't recall.   I didn't say it

21   didn't happen, but I can't recall that.

22   MR. HUR: All right.   Anything else on that before

23   I move on?

24   MR. KRICKBAUM: I had a slightly unrelated

25   question, Mr. President, but it is something you --

1   [0:06:59.0]

2   MR. HUR: -- presidency, did you consult these

3   materials relating to the Iran nuclear deal at any point?

4   Did you know that they were at the Penn Biden Center?

5   PRESIDENT BIDEN: No. And I, I don't recall

6   consulting anything having to do with any material with

7   regard to Iran.

8

9

10

11

12

13

14

15   MR. SISKEL: And, sir, just to clarify, that's

16   during your --

17   PRESIDENT BIDEN: Oh, that's just --

18   MR. SISKEL: That's (indiscernible 0:07:57.5) your

19   presidency, which they're not interested in.

20   MR. HUR: Right.

21   PRESIDENT BIDEN: No, I know, but I want to give

22   you context in my, my -- the depth of my engagement. And,

23   anyway.

24   MR. HUR: Okay. So let me ask a slightly

25   different question, but riffing off one I asked you before.

1   [1:20:23.9]

2   PRESIDENT BIDEN: And it may be -- I don't remember

3   the purpose of the meeting, but lots of times that I meet and

4   say, well, what do you guys think, you know, rather than just

5   selling something. And say, why do you think that would work,

6   et cetera. So I don't know what the topic was.

7   MR. HUR: Understood.

8   PRESIDENT BIDEN: And -- but it's not unusual to

9   have those meetings.

10   MR. HUR: Understood. Okay.

11   MR. BAUER: I just wanted to mention, I think

12   we're at 5 hours.

13   MR. HUR: Is that right?

14   MR. BAUER: It's 2 -- in fact, we're at 5 hours and

15   1 minute. Not that I -- not that we're keeping time on this.

16   MR. HUR: If you wouldn't mind, if you could

17   indulge us to just finish this line of questioning.

18   MR. BAUER: How much more time do you think you

19   would need?

20   MR. HUR: I really don't think I'll need more than

21   10 or 15 minutes on this.

22   MR. BAUER: I couldn't hear.

23   PRESIDENT BIDEN: 10 or 15 minutes.

24   MR. HUR: Yes, sir.

25   MR. HUR: And I'll do my best to make it closer --

DRAFT 93

[0:04:19.8]

    MR. HUR: -- refresh your recollection as to the purpose of these handwritten notes relating to the Iran nuclear deal, or your breakfast meeting with the senators the following day?

    MR. BAUER: Rob, just to be clear.

    PRESIDENT BIDEN: No.

    MR. BAUER: I'm a little confused, because if they're not the same documents --

    MR. HUR: Yes.

    MR. BAUER: -- what would be the basis of refreshing his recollection?

    MR. HUR: Well, if his response is that they do.

    MR. BAUER: Okay.

    MR. HUR: It doesn't refresh his recollection --

    MR. BAUER: Okay.

    PRESIDENT BIDEN: No, this doesn't refresh my recollection. But I'm sure the purpose of the meeting was to find out what the members of Congress thought about the Iran deal. I mean, that's why I'd been meeting with them about it. I assume that's why I was meeting with them about. I don't know what else -- it's contemporaneous, and I'm sitting down, and I'm having these discussions. And it says the people I'm meeting with are the people who would have interest. You know, Angus King and -- with the democrats. And --

```
1    [0:08:20.9]
2              MR. HUR:  Did you consult these materials during
3    your work on Promise Me, Dad with Mr. Zwonitzer?
4              PRESIDENT BIDEN:  I don't recall consulting any
5    material per se, that was in a folder or anything, for
6    Promise Me, Dad.
7              MR. HUR:  Mr. President, do you have any idea how
8    these documents relating to the Iran nuclear deal ended up in
9    these files that were recovered from the Penn Biden Center?
10             PRESIDENT BIDEN:  Other than when they were sent
11   to the Penn Biden Center, they followed on my vice
12   presidency, and it was one of the many subjects that were
13   talked about in my vice presidency.  So whatever materials
14   taken from the vice presidency over to the -- over to Penn
15   Biden Center, that's what -- I mean, there's a lot of things
16   I'm sure that got to the Penn Biden Center that are no
17   longer being actively discussed.
18             MR. HUR:  Anything else on this?  Okay.  I think I
19   came in under 10.
20             MR. BAUER:  You did.
21             MR. HUR:  Okay.
22             MR. BAUER:  You did.
23             MS. COTTON:  One minute under.
24             UNIDENTIFIED MALE SPEAKER:  One minute under
25   budget.
```

President Biden confuses world leaders with their long-dead predecessors

Feburary 7, 2024:

President Biden twice mixed up fellow heads of states with their much earlier predecessors.

First off, he confused French president Emmanuel Macron with Francois Mitterand, who died in 1996, during a rally address to supporters in Las Vegas, Nevada, while recounting a G7 meeting in Cornwall in June 2021.

President Biden: "Mitterrand from Germany – I mean, from France – looked at me and said, 'You know, what... why... how long you back for?"

Speaking subsequently in New York a few days later, he claimed to have discussed the Capitol riot with German chancellor Helmut Kohl, who passed away in 2017, four years before it took place.

He was thinking of Angela Merkel.

Source: Independent.UK

President Biden can't recall the terrorist group Hamas.

Feburary 7, 2024:

President Biden appeared unable to recall the name of the terror group being fought by Israel in Gaza, stumbling awkwardly over his words during a press conference at the White House.

Source: Independent.UK

President Biden mixes up Mexico and Egypt at surprise presser to address claims of memory loss.

Feburary 9, 2024:

President Joe Biden appeared to confuse Mexico with Egypt, in a press conference on Thursday called to refute allegations of his poor memory.

The president made reference to the ongoing conflict in the Middle East, saying:

President Biden: "The president of Mexico did not want to open up the gate to allow humanitarian material to get in. I talked to him. I convinced to open the gate."

Source: Independent.UK

President Biden flubs Capitol Riot date.

March 7, 2024:

President Biden briefly said the 2021 Capitol riot took place on July 6 before correcting himself and saying, "January 6."

Source: Fox News

President Biden can't recall the correct facts about his Uncle.

April 17, 2024:

President Biden twice suggested during a visit to a Scranton, Penn., World War II memorial honoring his uncle, Ambrose Finnegan, that his body may have been eaten—by people, saying, "[H]e got shot down in New Guinea, and they never found the body because there used to be a lot of cannibals, for real, in that part of the New Guinea." But the official military account of his death states that his Air Force plane crashed into the ocean off the coast of New Guinea and that neither his body nor the aircraft were recovered.

Source: Forbes

President Biden looks confused and mixes up words again during a speech

April 24, 2024:

President Biden: "Folks, in a sense, I don't know why we're surprised by Trump. How many times does he have to prove we can't be trusted?"

Mistakenly saying "we" instead of "he", Mr Biden accidentally lumped himself in with President Trump.

During the same speech, he also read off the "pause" command from the teleprompter.

President Biden: "I see an America where we defend democracy, not diminish it. I see an America where we protect freedoms, not take them away. I see an economy that grows a lot in the bottom up where the wealthy pay their fair share, so we can have child care, paid leave and so much more, and still reduce the federal deficit and increase economic folks. Imagine what we could do next. Four more years, pause."

President Biden makes up a memory.

April 26, 2024:

President Biden repeated a heavily disputed claim that he was arrested while standing on the porch with a Black family who was moving into Lynnfield, Delaware, as it was being desegregated. Protesters gathered outside, recalling to radio host Howard Stern he was "brought back" home by the police—previous fact-checks by multiple outlets into Biden's oft-repeated claim have unearthed newspaper articles from 1959 reporting arrests at protests outside two homes of Black families near where Biden was living at the time. Still, there's no evidence Biden was among those taken into custody.

Source: Forbes

President Biden gaffes at campaign fundraiser.

May 3, 2024:

"At a campaign fundraiser organized and attended largely by Asian American donors and lawmakers on Wednesday, President Joe Biden described three Asian countries, including U.S. ally Japan and an emerging partner, India, as "xenophobic."

Biden, who was crediting immigrants with fueling the American economy, went on to attribute 'xenophobia' as a reason the economies of Russia, China, Japan and India were struggling.

Except: India is one of the fastest growing economies in the world, whose gross domestic product grew at 8.4% in the final three months of 2023."

Source: USA Today

President Biden reads incorrectly off the teleprompter while hosting the Presidential Medal of Freedom.

May 4, 2024:

President Biden reads incorrectly off the teleprompter while hosting the Presidential Medal of Freedom.

President Biden: "I congratulate Presidential Freedom of Medal recipients."

President Biden also stutters while giving an introduction of a recipient.

President Biden: 'She's not only, she's not only the only person receiving this medal, she is a, uh, she is a, uh, you know..."

President Biden says "Last Name" during speech instead of the person's last name.

May 8, 2024:

President Biden: "My theology professor at the Catholic school I went to was a guy named Reilley, last name. And he had been drafted by the Green Bay Packers."

President Biden calls a basketball player a coach

May 9, 2024:

The president said Candace Parker—a two-time WNBA Most Valuable Player and Olympic gold medalist who retired from the Aces after 16 seasons in the league—"will be considered one of the greatest all-time coaches" while honoring the Aces for their 2023 WNBA championship win at the White House, according to a transcript of his remarks.

Source: TIME

President Biden Calls Kim Jong Un President Of South Korea

May 10, 2024:

In his most recent gaffe, President Joe Biden of the United States mistakenly referred to North Korean leader Kim Jong Un as the president of South Korea.

The blunder by the world leader happened when Biden focused on ex-President Donald Trump at a campaign event in Portola Valley, California. The Democratic candidate criticized his Republican opponent for his strong connections with the North Korean leader and Russian President Putin.

President Biden: "We'll never forget his love letters for the South Korean President Kim Jong Un or his admiration for Putin — what a great leader Putin is,"

Source: Times of India

CHAPTER 3: ANGER IS THE NEW NORM

In situations that require a detailed response, or when a person with the onset of cognitive decline is presented with a question in a social setting, it's common for them to feel angry and lash out as they cannot process everything at once.

In a speech, President Biden spazzes out on the lack of democracy in the world.

President Biden: "We have fewer democracies in the world today than we did fifteen years ago. Fewer. (starts to yell uncontrollably) Not more. Fewer!"

President Biden gets angry with a Fox News reporter.

Do you think inflation is a political liability?" Fox News's Peter Doocy asked as aides shooed reporters out of the White House East Room.

President Biden: "No, it's a great asset — more inflation. What a stupid son of a bitch."

President Biden snaps on father of daughter who was killed at Parkland High School.

July 11, 2022:

President Biden couldn't control his outburst regarding an outburst during his speech.

First, he yelled at a grieving father who lost his 17-year-old son in the February 14, 2018, massacre at a Florida high school.

President Biden: "Sit down! You'll hear what I have to say."

Source: New York Post

President Biden angry that he doesn't get enough credit.

March 17, 2024:

NBC News article states that behind the scenes, Biden has grown angry and anxious about re-election effort.

"Biden has long believed that he isn't getting sufficient credit for an economy that has created 15 million new jobs. Surrounded by protective aides who want to minimize the chances of a flub, the 81-year-old president has chafed at restraints that he sees as counter to his natural instincts as a retail politician, a third person familiar with internal discussions said.

He has felt cocooned at times and has been eager to get out more, meet voters face-to-face and take the fight directly to Trump, said the third person and a fourth also familiar with the matter who, like others, spoke on condition of anonymity to discuss campaign strategy and the president's private views."

Source: NBC News

What does the mainstream liberal public think about President Biden's lack of memory and angry outbursts? They love it! They say it reminds them of an old-school "grandfather" approach.

A 2023 Reddit forum is actually dedicated to how "cool" President Biden is for being an angry old guy who forgets he's actually President at-times.

Juggerginge · 10mo ago

Biden's challenge to his aides to explain things in simple terms is so good. Teaching highly successful and intelligent people to dumb down their policy explanations if key to getting the average person to both care and understand it properly

⬆ 383 ⬇   💬 Reply   ⬆ Share   ⋯

➕ 47 more replies

PassTheChronic · 10mo ago

Why it matters: The private eruptions paint a more complicated picture of Biden as a manager and president than his carefully cultivated image as a kindly uncle who loves Aviator sunglasses and ice cream.

ThugLyfeBiden.JPG

⬆ 142 ⬇   💬 Reply   ⬆ Share   ⋯

➕ 1 more reply

Zenning2 OP · 10mo ago

Zoom out: Biden's temper comes in the form of angry interrogations rather than erratic tantrums.

He'll grill aides on topics until it's clear they don't know the answer to a question — a routine that some see as meticulous and others call "stump the chump" or "stump the dummy."

Being yelled at by the president has become an internal initiation ceremony in this White House, aides say — if Biden doesn't yell at you, it could be a sign he doesn't respect you.

Based

⊖ ⬆ 429 ⬇   💬 Reply   ⬆ Share   ⋯

Steak_Knight · 10mo ago

"Look, fat, do you know or don't you?"

⬆ 226 ⬇   💬 Reply   ⬆ Share   ⋯

twdarkeh · 10mo ago

Everything in this article makes me love Biden more.

⊖ ⬆ 185 ⬇   💬 Reply   ⬆ Share   ⋯

> **BBQ_HaX0r** · 10mo ago
>
> I think that's the point. This is an article that at first glance seems like a criticism but is actually addressing one of this biggest criticisms (too old, not engaged, aloof, etc).
>
> ⬆ 56 ⬇   💬 Reply   ⬆ Share   ⋯
>
> ⊕ 1 more reply

UntiedStatMarinCrops · 10mo ago · Edited 10mo ago

It seems like these aides came out with this information for this reason alone, pretty much:

> Some Biden aides think the president would be better off occasionally displaying his temper in public as a way to assuage voter concerns that the 80-year-old president is disengaged and too old for the office.

Edit: this also reminds me of THE BEST leader I've ever served under during my time in the Marine Corps. Lt. Colonel Harrison Strom. Man was hard on us and yelled at us quite a bit, but man, I was so motivated under his leadership that I was going to reenlist. I would have followed him to hell and back.

Edit: also want to add how badass this dude was in top of being the best leader I've ever served. He served enlisted and fought in the Iraq War, got out and went to college, joined as a commissioned officer once he joined again, did badass shit with MARSOC (now called Marine Raiders), and then become our commanding officer, and did something officers don't really do: got promoted in front of the entire unit he was in charge of (usually officers only get promoted in front of other officers). He eventually left and served the remainder of his time working at MARSOC. He would yell a lot, but he was also very compassionate and understanding, and didn't tolerate bullshit like hazing and even promoted equality while every other Sgt Major bitched about women being in the military.

⊖ ⬆ 185 ⬇   💬 Reply   ⬆ Share   ⋯

> **Electrical-Swing-935** · 10mo ago
>
> Can you describe at all what about his leadership motivated you so much?
>
> ⬆ 44 ⬇   💬 Reply   ⬆ Share   ⋯

(It's tiring being so cool)

CHAPTER 4: LOST OF FUNCTIONS

President Biden is old. He's 81 and still kicking, and that's a good thing. What's the bad thing? He falls constantly; he can't hold himself up; instead, he has to prop himself up with others or inanimate objects. He also can't control bodily functions and has trouble eating certain foods because of the chance of a mishap.

President Biden falls down the steps of airforce one three times.

March 19, 2021:

According to ABCNEWS: Biden 'just fine' after tripping 3 times jogging up steps to Air Force One - ABC News (go.com)

"Each time, he placed his left hand down to catch himself while holding onto the railing with his right hand."

"He eventually fell onto his left knee midway up the steps."

"As he stood up, Biden paused and appeared to adjust the bottom of his pant leg before continuing to lightly jog and then walk up the remainder of the steps, then turning to give a salute before entering the cabin."

White House principal deputy press secretary Karine Jean-Pierre told reporters aboard Air Force One that the president was doing "just great" and blamed the incident on wind gusts.

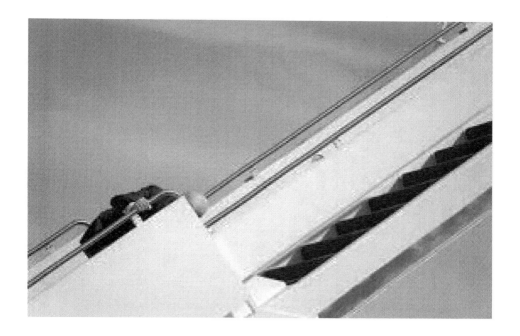

Joe Biden stumbles on steps of Air Force One

President Biden falls asleep at COP26 Summit in 2021.

"For at least 50 seconds of recorded time, during a speech he's listening to, President Biden sits with his arms crossed, in a position of sleep, as his eyes are closed." (An assistant wakes him up).

President Biden shits himself in front of Duchess Camilla at the 2021 COP26 Summitt.

The duchess "hasn't stopped talking about" Biden's fart, an "informed source" stated.

Source: Politico

President Biden shits himself at a meeting with Pope Francis at the Vatican.

While on a visit to the Vatican, President Biden is said to have shit himself and had to be escorted to a nearby facility to be cleaned up.

There is no confirmed source on this headline but I included it to showcase a possibility of truth when you add in his past remarks and loss of functions - he barely has control over anything.

According to The-Sun.com: "Conservative strategist and commentator Amy Tarkanian tweeted: 'The word around Rome is that Biden's meeting with the Pope was unusually long because Biden had a bit of a 'bathroom incident' at the Vatican and it had to be addressed prior to him leaving.

'I know we often joke about this but this is the actual rumor going around Rome now.'

There is no evidence to support these wild claims, Meaww reports.

Biden appeared to apologize to reporters for keeping them waiting during a press briefing.

The bumbling president said: 'We were playing with elevators.'

The Vatican said that Friday's meeting lasted for around 75 minutes and then another 15 minutes were spent for photos and exchanging gifts.

Pope Francis met with former President Donald Trump for 30 minutes in 2017 and Barack Obama for 52 minutes in 2014."

Source: Unconfirmed/Rumor

President Biden falls off his bicycle.

Yes. He fell off his bicycle. Below is a snippet of an article explaining what "happened."

June 18, 2022:

"President Joe Biden is "fine," after falling off his bike Saturday during a ride in a state park near his home in Rehoboth Beach, Delaware, a White House official said.

No medical attention is needed, the official added in a statement released to reporters traveling with the President.

"As the President said, his foot got caught on the pedal while dismounting and he is fine. No medical attention is needed. The President looks forward to spending the rest of the day with his family," the official said.
Biden took a tumble when he was finishing a bike ride alongside first lady Jill Biden.

The President deviated from the group as he biked over to a crowd that had gathered nearby. Biden came to a stop and appeared to get his foot caught on the pedal while trying to dismount.

"I got my foot caught" on the toe cage, Biden told reporters traveling with him later. "I'm good."

Source: CNN

<u>President Biden exhausted and barely standing up while giving a speech in Vietnam.</u>

September 10, 2023:

"I don't know about you, but I'm going to go to bed."

President Biden leaves the podium at "The Global Fund" speech and looks visibly confused on where to go or where he's at.

September 21, 2022:

(He walks with both hands in front of him, like he's about to give an invisible person a double handshake. He then looks around aimlessly while making hand motions to someone off-stage. He then stands, looking around for someone to get him.)

President Biden stumbles on steps of airforce one on way back from Ukraine visit.

Feburary 23, 2023:

According to the Independent.UK:

"Joe Biden appeared to stumble making his way up the stairs to Air Force One as the president embarked on a return flight back from his surprise visit to Ukraine and Poland."

"In footage of the incident, the president appeared to trip about halfway up the steps, before regaining his balance and waving then getting inside the plane"

President Biden stumbles at Air Force Graduation.

June 1, 2023:

President Biden took another rather worrying tumble while on stage at the Air Force Academy graduation ceremony that same month.

The president delivered the commencement address at the event and stayed on stage as graduates were handed their diplomas.

As he walked off, he then stumbled and fell to the ground.

He was helped up by Air Force officials and appeared to point at a nearby sandbag as the reason for the mishap.

White House communications director Ben LaBolt later tweeted that he was "fine" and that "there was a sandbag on stage while he was shaking hands".

Source: Independent.UK

President Biden almost slips exiting Air Force One... again.

September 26, 2023:

President Biden, 80, slipped and nearly tumbled down a 14-step staircase while exiting Air Force One on Tuesday just hours after it was revealed that the President is working with a physical therapist and using shorter stairs to avoid further trip-ups.

Source: New York Post

A special report on by Axios:

April 28, 2024:

Journalist Alex Thompson stated that President Biden and his staff had changed his routine walk to and from Marine One (helicopter).

His staff is now accompanying him, walking alongside him. They have also shortened the staircase to Air Force One.

"Biden, 80, has stumbled on the tall stairs more than once. The short stairs have the distinct advantage of moving most of Biden's ascent into Air Force One out of public view. But for those who have noticed the shift, it also draws attention to one of Biden's greatest political liabilities as he seeks reelection: his age."

Source: NPR.org

CHAPTER 5: THE ENABLERS

President Biden's recent campaign tactics resemble the 1989 comedy blockbuster "Weekend at Bernie's" more than anything like a political movement. Why is he the only choice for the Democrats, and why are so many close to him okay with enabling him? One answer. President Donald Trump. But is there more to it? What are the underlying reasons for these tactics, and what do they say about our political discourse?

There is a palpable fear of political warfare if anyone who doesn't appear 'feeble' is put forward. While his gaffes and functionality are undeniably problematic, they are shielded from an actual debate and from the public eye. The power to enable his memory loss and loss of functions is building up to the 2024 Presidential election.

President Biden's failing memory gives him the ability to get out of a potential Federal charge in relation to anything illegal that took place before, during, or after Biden's Presidency. The U.S. Government clearly gave this perception when Special Counsel Robert Hur declined to prosecute President Joe Biden on the same charges President Trump is facing in a Federal court: Mishandling classified records and files after leaving political office.

President Biden escaped going to court simply because he is an "elderly man with a poor memory."

Below is a passage of an article from The New Yorker:

"Hur had completed his report on whether President Joe Biden had mishandled classified documents—he had declined to prosecute Biden but had impugned the President's memory in the process—and members of both parties were furious. "I knew it was going to be unpleasant," he told me this past week, "but the level of vitriol —it's hard to know exactly how intense that's going to be until the rotten fruit is being thrown at you."

Hell, they even gave President Trump's Federal investigation an offical operations name: PLASMIC ECHO

"This document contains information that is restricted to case participants," the document reads. It adds, "PLASMIC ECHO; Mishandling Classified or National Defense Information, Unknown Subject; Sensitive Investigation Matter."

During the interview with Special Counsel Robert Hur, President Biden answers questions but also can't recall key moments in his life.

Starting off the interview:

Robert Hur: "On the topic of cooperation, you know, as Federal prosecutors, we do assess cooperation at the end of an investigation. Obviously, your willingness to sit for this interview today and tomorrow and answer our questions is part of this cooperation. It's obviously very important you answer our questions truthfully. And we appreciate very much your willingness, and we hope that you will be able -- that you'll put forth your best efforts and really try to get your best recollection in response to the questions we ask, because I acknowledge that some of the questions we are asking relate to events that happened years ago."

President Biden: "I'm a young man, so it's not a problem."

When asked about his son's death, Beau Biden and the date it happened:

President Biden: "And so what was happening, though — what month did Beau die? Oh God, May 30,".

An attorney from the White House counsel's office interjected to say "2015," a year then echoed by a second unidentified speaker.

President Biden: "Was it 2015, he had died?"

President Biden is confused and pauses.

President Biden: "And what's happened in the meantime is that Trump gets elected in November of 2017?"

Two people corrected him, saying, "2016."

President Biden: "2016. All right, so — why do I have 2017 here?" (referring to a peice of paper).

President Biden issued a press conference in reaction to Special Counsel Robert Hur's report that he has a bad memory and is old.

In response to how he could not remember his son's death date or the year associated with Trump's Presidency.

President Biden: "How in the hell dare he raise that?"

Politico developed an article entitled:

Why Late Night Shows Won't Roast Joe Biden

"Colbert's ultra-friendly exchanges with Biden, Obama, and Clinton as emcee of the largest Democratic fundraiser ever — it raised a whopping $26 million for Biden's reelection effort — were emblematic of a new era in late-night comedy. It's more proudly partisan. More one-sided. More cautious in its targets. And it's generally soft on Biden.

By any metric, Biden is a rich vein of material for late night or sketch comics. He arrived in the White House with a hard-earned reputation as a gaffe machine. The oldest President ever, he was first elected to the Senate during the era of eight-track tapes and rotary telephones. Since his ascendancy to the White House, he has fairly consistently stumbled over his own words, mixed up the names of world leaders and countries, and even physically stumbled on stage himself, tripping and falling at a U.S. Air Force graduation. His speaking style can be jarring: He can sound something like an old-timey preacher, delivering surprising anecdotes while vacillating between a yell and a whisper."

Source: Politico

Biden is trying to turn his age from punching bag to punchline

On his age, Biden now trying to show he's in on the joke

"Joe Biden once joked that, when he knocked on doors while running for senate as a 29-year-old, people would mistake him for a newspaper delivery boy, or perhaps someone wanting to cut their lawn.

The crowd laughed.

And now, as the 80-year-old incumbent president begins his fourth and final presidential campaign, he once again is turning toward questions of his age. But where he once was defensive, now he tries to be good-humored. Where he once rebuffed questions about being the oldest president and any accompanying suggestions of frailty, now he embraces them and argues that with age comes wisdom."

Source: The Washington Post

Why the mainstream public and the media doesn't care about President Biden's age.

No one cares if the media is one-sided with its comedy routines.

This has become the norm, the day-to-day thought process of the radical left and its media personalities. They hate President Donald Trump so much that they will prop up a false idol to complete their wants and needs. They are "They". They rule the things you and I see each day, as they have a stronghold on the media and almost anything that profits in liberal cities and states.

The U.S. Government is actively shielding the public's view from the President as they will not release the audio from Special Counsel Robert Hur's interview from October 8th and 9th, 2023. The written transcript is available online, but critics say the audio will give a better understanding of President Biden's cognitive abilities, word speech, etc.

"The Justice Department notified Congress on Thursday that it will not comply with a subpoena for audio recordings of President Biden's interview with former Special Counsel Robert Hur.

In an 11-page letter, Assistant Attorney General Carlos Uriarte rejected claims from House Judiciary Chairman Jim Jordan (R-Ohio) and Oversight Chairman James Comer (R-Ky.) that the recordings contain information relevant to the Republican-led impeachment inquiry into the 81-year-old President."

Source: New York Post

On May 5, 2024, I performed a test on MSN'S Artififical Intelligence program called "Copilot with GPT-4".

This is a search engine that takes key-words and presents a summary based on A.I.'s interpretation of that key-word or question.

I typed in "Biden's bad memory" and "Trump's bad memory."

Here are the results.

Biden's bad memory results:

"Since a report released by special counsel Robert Hur described President Joe Biden as an "elderly man with a poor memory," there have been significant misperceptions about the cognitive changes associated with aging. The report noted that President Biden couldn't recall defining milestones in his own life, such as when his son Beau died or when he served as vice president. However, neurologists emphasize that forgetting names of acquaintances or having difficulty remembering dates from the past, especially when under stress, can simply be part of normal aging. Almost every older individual experiences trouble remembering people's names, and this type of forgetfulness doesn't necessarily predict memory disorders [1].

Dr. Paul Newhouse, clinical core leader for the Vanderbilt Alzheimer's Disease Research Center, explains that if you asked him when his mother passed away, he couldn't necessarily tell you the exact year because it was many years ago. Forgetting names is a common complaint as people age. Similarly, Dr. Dennis Selkoe, co-director of the Ann Romney Center for Neurologic Diseases at Brigham and Women's Hospital in Boston, agrees that forgetting names doesn't provide much insight into potential memory problems. Stress and lack of sleep can interfere with memory, regardless of age.

While it's normal for older brains to have more difficulty retaining new information and retrieving it, mental processes like decision-making and judgment can actually improve with age. Wisdom can increase due to a greater backlog of experiences, allowing individuals to make better decisions based on their accumulated knowledge. So, while President Biden may occasionally forget names or specific details, it doesn't necessarily indicate a significant memory disorder.

Remember that only a person's doctor or neurologist can make a proper diagnosis regarding memory disorders, not outside observers. If you have any other questions or need further information, feel free to ask!"

Trump's bad memory results:

There has been speculation about former President Donald Trump's memory and cognitive abilities. Some mental health professionals have raised concerns, while others have defended him. Let's explore some perspectives:

Evidence of Dementia:

Dr. Lance Dodes, a retired Harvard Medical School professor, claims there is "overwhelming" evidence that Trump is suffering from dementia. He points to Trump's confusion about reality, such as confusing Barack Obama with Joe Biden.

New York psychologist Suzanne Lachmann has observed behavior in Trump that is consistent with dementia, including forgetting how sentences began and creating incomprehensible word salads.

Cognitive Test Bragging:

In 2020, Trump bragged about the results of a cognitive test, claiming he had "a good memory" and was "cognitively there" during an interview with Fox News2.

However, this self-assessment does not necessarily provide a comprehensive picture of his cognitive abilities.
Anonymous White House Insider:

An anonymous senior government official claimed that Trump regularly struggles to remember what he has said or been told.

This suggests memory challenges, although the source remains anonymous.

Psychologists' Concerns:

Mental health professionals have expressed concern about Trump's verbal functioning and cognitive decline. In 2018, over 70 psychologists urged Trump's physician to administer a cognitive exam during his physical examination.

These concerns highlight the need for further evaluation.

In summary, opinions on Trump's memory vary, but it's clear that his cognitive abilities have been a topic of discussion. Keep in mind that this information reflects various viewpoints, and a definitive assessment would require a thorough evaluation by medical experts.

My analysis: The A.I. algorithm has a support system that benefits President Biden more than President Trump.

Here's a short list of the main enablers of President Biden's failing memory:

Jill Biden

She's the First Lady of The United States and his wife. She is with him the most and clearly knows everything that's wrong with him.

Carlos Felipe Uriarte

As Assistant Attorney General, he's moving up the ranks and following orders. He's preventing anyone on the outside from looking in.

Secret Service Agents

Their job is to protect the President, not question his mental capabilities, as the public elected him in a democracy. They see everything, they protect him from mishaps and gaffes. They know the truth and how bad off President Biden is with everyday tasks.

Julie Chávez Rodríguez

Her job is to get President Biden reflected. As his campaign manager for the 2024 election, she has to lie and maintain face with the outside world as they prop him up to seem sound of mind.

Karine Jean-Pierre

This one changes regularly, as this job doesn't last long. Her job as White House Press Secretary is to lie, make the Presiden't gaffes seem innocent, and maintain a communication with selected media organizations that meets the White House agenda.

CHAPTER 6: THE PERCEPTION OF THE PRESIDENCY

For one second, forget the name of this book and the subject matter. Let's say President Biden is entirely healthy and sound of mind - with the perception, take a look at everything you've read and ask yourself this:

How do these many mistakes make the United States look?

Feeble.

Weak.

Vulnerable.

Our President is the face of the country, but right now, that face is asleep most of the time or falling off an airplane somewhere. The projection he gives is pitiful. We need a strong leader who can articulate his words and knows what he wants to achieve.

Below are news articles and instances where other countries have caught President Biden's memory lapses.

Sky News Australia

Biden stumbles through a gaffe-laden speech.

President Biden: "Look at what we did recently when Israel was attacked and, I made it clear to the Israelis, don't move on Haifa.

The city the President meant to say is "Rafah."

Hindustan Times: Pakistan

Biden's New Gaffe: Asks Americans To Choose Freedom Or Democracy

(Squinting at the teleprompter)

President Biden: "Are you ready to choose freedom over democracy? Because that's America."

(Crown erupts with praise and applause)

(President Biden is often seen squinting or closing his eyes during speeches).

Italian TV MOCKS Joe Biden In 'Hilarious' Sketch Of President's On-Stage Gaffes

"In a recent viral skit from an Italian TV show, the cognitive abilities of President Joe Biden were put under the spotlight once again. The comedic interpretation of Biden struggling on stage outside the White House has sparked a debate on social media about his mental state and ability to lead the country."

Biden made 148 gaffes so far in 2024

According to the Daily Caller, President Biden made 148 mistakes in public statements between January 1 and April 24.

President Biden stuttered or lost his wording 118 times in the same period.

A team of "fixers" who are editors work to correct President Biden's statements when they go out in an official transcript or when the statement needs more clarity.

Some notable moments from 2024 include:

Laken Riley's mother slams Biden for fumbling murdered nursing student's name at State of the Union: 'Pathetic'

"The heartbroken mother of Georgia nursing student Laken Riley slammed President Biden for fumbling her daughter's name during the State of Union speech — calling him "pathetic" for the slip.

'Biden does not even KNOW my child's name – it [sic] pathetic!' Allyson Philips wrote Friday in response to a comment on a Facebook post celebrating the passage of the Laken Riley Act.

'If you are going to say her name (even when forced to do so), at least say the right name!' she insisted.

The grieving mother also wrote 'Amen!' underneath a comment that called Biden "a disgrace of a president."

Source: New York Post

Biden slips up while defending himself.

The 388-page report set off a political firestorm, resulting in a clumsy response from the White House and the President himself. Biden angrily rejected Hur's claim, saying Thursday night in a press conference he felt questions about Beau weren't "any of their damn business."

The President got choked up while showing a rosary he was wearing on his wrist in memory of Beau, then thundered, "I don't need anyone to remind me when he passed away."

If Biden had left it at that, that might be what people remembered about the news conference. Instead, Biden wound up walking right into the stereotype laid out by Hur when he mistakenly said that President Abdel Fattah El-Sisi of Egypt was the "president of Mexico" while answering a question about current hostage negotiations with Israel and Hamas.

Source: NPR.org

Even those in public office and business don't want President Biden to run again, calling on his enablers to stop their propaganda.

Congressman Dean Phillips from Minnesota posted about

President Biden's memory on X.com, and it quickly went viral.

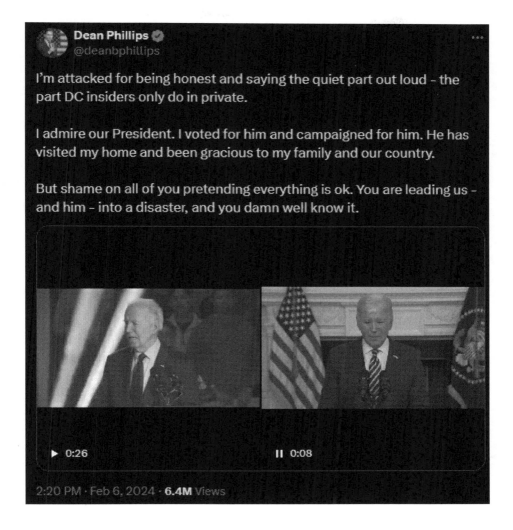

In the videos President Biden rambles on and on while making mistake after mistake.

First video:

President Biden: "Right after I was elected I went to what they call a G7 meeting, all the NATO leaders. I was in, I was in, south of England. And I sat down, and I said, 'America's back.' Emmanuel from Germany, I mean from France, looked at me and said, and said, 'You know, you know, how long are you back for?'

Second video:

President Biden: "There's been some movement, and I don't wanna, I don't wanna, (pauses) (mumbles) (squints eyes) let me choose my words. (Takes a deep breath). There's some movement. There's been a response from the uh, the, the, there's been a response... from... the opposition. But uh, it, it, yes, I'm sorry, from Hamas, but it seems to be uh, a little over the top, we're not sure where it is."

Dean Phillips ✔
@deanbphillips

In 2011, I hosted then VP Biden at my home. Most notable was his empathy and kindness to my daughters and the catering staff, with whom he sat and had ice cream (surprise-surprise). His decency and wisdom were rarities in politics then, and even more so today.

Over a decade later, the only thing that has changed is time - which slows all of us down a bit, including presidents.

I ran for Congress in 2018 to resist Donald Trump, I was trapped in the Capitol in 2021 because of Donald Trump, and I ran for President in 2024 to resist Donald Trump again - because Americans were demanding an alternative, and democracy demands options.

But it is clear that alternative is not me. And it is clear that Joe Biden is OUR candidate and OUR opportunity to demonstrate what type of country America is and intends to be.

To all who supported my effort, thank you. We will continue the important work to ensure a more responsive, democratic, and generationally diverse political system. But today, in light of the stark reality we face, I ask you join me in mobilizing, energizing, and doing everything you can to help keep a man of decency and integrity in the White House. That's Joe Biden.

Let's lead with invitation, not confrontation, to welcome Haley supporters, Trump supporters, and Uncommitted supporters to get this done. It's our calling, it's our legacy, and it's our time. Onward with joy and patriotism! 🤍🇺🇸

CHAPTER 7: THE 25TH AMENDMENT

There's no way President Biden can make it another four years and serve our country effectively. Suppose he somehow escapes the 2024 Presidential election with a victory. In that case, there are a few options the Democrats might try to enact to get him to relinquish power and get someone in the Presidency who has no chance of winning an election (Vice President Harris). The Twenty-fifth Amendment to The United States Constitution gives power to remove a President who does not provide sufficient support for the office.

Unforeseen emergencies can include the kidnapping of the President and "political emergencies" such as impeachment. Traits like unpopularity, incompetence, impeachable conduct, poor judgment, or laziness might not necessarily constitute inability, but if they reach a level where they hinder the President from fulfilling their constitutional duties, they could still be regarded as inability, even without a formal medical diagnosis. Furthermore, a President who displayed disabling traits when they were elected cannot be shielded from a declaration of inability.

Section 3 allows for the voluntary transfer of presidential authority to the vice president (for example, in anticipation of a medical procedure) by the President declaring in writing to be unable to discharge the powers and duties of the Presidency. The vice president then assumes those powers and duties as acting President; the vice president does not become President, and the President remains in office, although without authority. The President regains those powers and duties upon declaring, in writing, to be again able to discharge them.

Section 4 outlines the conditions under which the Vice President assumes the powers and duties of the office. Whenever the Vice President and a majority of either the principal officers of the executive departments or of such other body as Congress may by law provide, transmit to the President pro tempore of the Senate and the Speaker of the House of Representatives their written declaration that the President is unable to discharge the powers and duties of his office, the Vice President shall immediately assume the powers and duties of the office as Acting President. This provision ensures a smooth transition of power in case of the President's inability to discharge his duties.

After the President transmits to the President pro tempore of the Senate and the Speaker of the House of Representatives a written declaration that they are no longer unable to perform their duties, they will resume their powers and responsibilities. However, if the Vice President and a majority of either the principal officers of the executive department or of such other body as Congress may by law provide, transmit a written declaration within four days to the President pro tempore of the Senate and the Speaker of the House of Representatives stating that the President is unable to perform their duties, then they will not resume their powers and duties.

If the President cannot carry out the office's duties and

responsibilities, Congress plays a critical role in deciding the matter. Congress must assemble within forty-eight hours to determine if it is not in session. If Congress receives a written declaration regarding the President's incapacity and does not assemble, it has twenty-one days to do so. If Congress determines by a two-thirds vote of both Houses that the President is incapable of carrying out the powers and duties of his office, the Vice President will continue as Acting President. If Congress fails to reach a two-thirds vote, the President will resume the powers and duties of his office. This process emphasizes the democratic nature of our system, where the representatives of the people ultimately make the decision.

Congressman Ken Buck introduces a resolution claiming President is incapable of executing duties – but it has little chance of success.

February 26, 2024:

Buck's resolution states: "President Biden has been televised wandering aimlessly at events and frequently speaks publicly in an incoherent and indiscernible manner and has repeatedly fallen while walking upstairs."

In a statement about his resolution, Buck said: "The Hur report officially addressed what many Americans have long witnessed with their own eyes – that President Biden is no longer fit to successfully discharge the critical duties of his office."

Source: The Guardian

CHAPTER 8: THE 2024 ELECTION

The matchup is President Trump versus President Biden. In one corner, an aging man that gets angry quickly and sometimes forgets things. In the other corner, an aging man that gets angry speedily and often forgets things. Your job is to decipher the effects of growing old and the effects of severe cognitive decline.

President Trump will be 78 years old by the time November 5, 2024 rolls around. President Biden will turn 82 years old two weeks after the election. Every day is an ongoing battle not to forget things when you're that old, but that isn't the only problem these two have going for themselves.

Take age out of the equation, and most of President Trump's word mix-ups can be attributed to misunderstandings of those who hear the words or just plain old age. President Biden's word mix-ups are worrisome and demean the office of the Presidency with every incident.

According to an NBC News poll, voters main issues with each candidate are as follows:

President Trump: His criminal trial.

ident Biden: His age.

An ABC News poll showed that 59% of voters believe both candidates are too old and shouldn't run for office. The reality has settled, and we are both running for political office. President Trump isn't perfect; he's facing criminal charges and has a personality that can be a turn-off. One thing President Trump doesn't do? He doesn't constantly fall down the steps of Air Force One, he doesn't mumble sentences during speeches, and he can navigate the ins and outs of a stage.

Some people, though, don't care about age; most of those people are old themselves, as this interview shows blow:

"Regardless of the reasons, age is an issue in this election. Seventy-one-year-old Norma Rodrigues of Miami, Florida, says that's not right."

"Just as age shouldn't be an issue in any workplace when it doesn't affect capacity, it shouldn't matter in politics either. Rather, we should vote on traits like character, empathy, and trustworthiness."

Source: VOANews.com

The tables are stacked against Trump. I wrote this book not to make money, but to inform. After you read this book, give it to someone, or buy them a copy. Pass the word around, leave reviews and support what you believe in. We are all in the same battle and President Biden is a disgrace as the face of this great nation we call THE UNITED STATES OF AMERICA.

To combat President Biden's inability to lead the country, a criminal trial has been established against President Trump. If President Biden's memory loss is at the core of his downfall, they just guard him from public appearances where President Trump will also be in attendance.

President Biden's team has done a good job at maintaining their puppet, but it's finally at a point where he's been allowed to "come out and play." President Trump will be in and out of courthouses, defending his honor and name. This will cut down on campaign trips and his ability to challenge President Biden.

As you've read throughout this book, President Biden's staff has taken precautions to deal with his age and loss of memory. They can't keep him from giving speeches since that's part of his job. They know that slip-ups and mental decline are not taken seriously by the mainstream media (another reason I wrote this book). As you've also read, they applaud and cheer President Biden after his memory lapses! These people are delusional; they're just as bad as him.

Wait.

You want more ten more examples? You need this book to be a little bit longer for your plane ride or evening relaxation?

1. During a speech in July 2021, Biden said, "We've seen incredible progress over the past 10 years, uh, uh, over the past 15 months. Uh, we've seen, uh, a lotta progress."

2. In September 2020, Biden said, "COVID has taken this year, just since the outbreak, has taken more than 100 years. Look, here's, the lives, it's just, it's, I mean, think about it."

3. During a speech in March 2021, Biden struggled with his

teleprompter, stating, "I'm, I'm gonna lose track here, we're gonna get in trouble. But, um, anyway..."

4. In a speech in February 2021, Biden struggled to pronounce the word "discrimination," saying, "The pandemic has, uh, disproportionately, uh, affected, uh, communities of color, uh, exacerbating, uh, systemic, uh, discrimi... uh, uh, disparate impacts, uh, health outcomes."

5. During a speech in April 2021, Biden stumbled over his words while discussing infrastructure, saying, "We're gonna talk about, uh, uh, what, um, uh, kind of, uh, infrastructure, um, uh, you know, can't just build, uh, everything, uh, you need... um... need to build."

6. During a CNN town hall in February 2021, Biden paused briefly and corrected himself while saying, "Uh, when I'm... when I... when I'm in, in, in, in... places like... uh... uh... uh... uh... uh... uh... uh..."

7. In June 2021, Biden aid, "I've been here a number of times... Last time was, uh, I think, all the way back in 2014, but I've been here before that."

8. March 2021: During a speech on the American Rescue Plan, President Biden stumbled over his words while reading from the teleprompter. He said, "In the weeks that this bill has been discussed and debated, it's clear that an overwhelming percentage of the American people..." before continuing with his speech.

9. March 2021: While discussing COVID-19 response efforts, Biden muttered, "We're sending a clear message to... to... Iran."

10. In December 2020, Biden struggled to remember the name of the Defense Department's cybersecurity agency, referring to it as "that outfit."

And one more thing. With the election on the way: 10 issues that President Biden faces.

1.Afghanistan Withdrawal Timing: Critics argue that the timing and execution of the withdrawal from Afghanistan led to chaos and the swift Taliban takeover.

2. Border Crisis Management: Some believe that Biden's approach to immigration and border security has exacerbated the situation at the southern border.

3. Inflation Concerns: Biden's economic policies have faced scrutiny, with concerns raised about rising inflation rates.

4. Energy Policy: Critics argue that some of Biden's energy policies, such as halting the Keystone XL pipeline, have negatively impacted jobs and energy independence.

5. COVID-19 Response: While praised for vaccine distribution, some criticize aspects of the pandemic response, such as inconsistent messaging on booster shots and mask mandates.

6. Supply Chain Issues: The administration has faced criticism for not adequately addressing supply chain disruptions, leading to shortages of various goods.

7. Tax Proposals: Biden's tax proposals, including potential increases for high-income individuals and corporations, have sparked debate over their potential economic impact.

8. Infrastructure Bill Negotiations: The lengthy negotiations over the infrastructure bill raised questions about the administration's ability to navigate bipartisan cooperation.

9. Russia-Ukraine Relations: Biden's approach to dealing with Russia and supporting Ukraine has drawn both praise and criticism for its effectiveness.

10. Crime and Public Safety: Some argue that Biden's approach to addressing rising crime rates and public safety concerns has been insufficient.

Made in the USA
Columbia, SC
28 April 2025

57269480R00057